BANGKOK

CITY OF ANGELS

Photography by Bill Wassman

Text by Joe Cummings

PERIPLUS

Published by Periplus Editions, with editorial office at 130 Joo Seng Road
#06-01, Singapore 368357. www.periplus.com

Copyright © 2005 Periplus Editions (HK) Ltd
ALL RIGHTS RESERVED
ISBN 0-7946-0128-6
Printed in Singapore

This book is dedicated to the memory of Bill Wassman who passed away in March
2003. Despite battling against cancer, Bill kept on traveling and doing what he
loved—shooting pictures—until the last week of his life.

All photographs by Bill Wassman except the following:
Luca Invernizzi Tettoni: Pages 4, 10, 11, 12, 13, 15, 16, 17, 20, 21, 24, 25, 27, 29, 30, 31,
32, 36, 37, 38, 41, 47, 51, 53, 60, 62, 69, 71, 72 (top left, bottom left and bottom right),
73 (top left, top right and bottom right), 76 (bottom left), 77 (top left and top right),
84, 85, 86, 87, 91, 95.

Masano Kawana: Page 6

Distributors
North America, Latin America and Europe Tuttle Publishing
364 Innovation Drive, North Clarendon, VT 05759-9436, USA
Tel: (802) 773 8930, Fax: (802) 526 6993, E-mail: info@tuttlepublishing.com

Asia Pacific Berkeley Books Pte Ltd
130 Joo Seng Road #06-01, Singapore 368357
Tel: (65) 6280 3320, Fax: (65) 6280 6290, E-mail: inquiries@periplus.com.sg

Japan and Korea Tuttle Publishing
Yaekari Building, 3F, 5-4-12 Osaki, Shinagawa-ku, Tokyo 141-0032
Tel: (813) 5437 6171, Fax: (813) 5437 0755, E-mail: tuttle-sales@gol.com

Front endpaper: A mural depicting a battle scene from Bangkok's past. Murals depict-
ing pivotal moments in the city's history were often painted on temple walls.
Back endpaper: This mural of early shophouses shows part of what daily life was like
for Bangkok's early immigrants.
Right: Giant ogre-like figures known as yak guard the grounds of many larger Bangkok
temples.
Opposite: Wat Benjamabophit, more commonly known in English as the 'Marble
Temple' because its walls and floors are built of white Carrara marble.

CONTENTS

"He wanted to go to the East, and his fancy was rich with pictures of Bangkok and Shanghai, and the ports of Japan: he pictured to himself palm-trees and skies blue and hot, dark-skinned people, pagodas, the scents of the Orient intoxicated his nostrils. His heart but with passionate desire for the beauty and the strangeness of the world."

— Somerset Maugham

THAILAND'S MEGATROPOLIS

Bangkok–the name explodes off the tongue, filling the mind with steamy images of the archetypal Southeast Asian metropolis. Emerging from the air-conditioned airport, the thick, jasmine-scented air immediately envelops your body, and the oceanic reverberation of distant traffic fills your ears. Your heart beats perceptibly faster, sensing that this is a place you'll not easily forget.

Swept along by the vehicular current into the heart of the capital, you soon find yourself lodged in a labyrinth that draws together the essence of everything that is sacred and profane in Thailand. Turn left and enter one world, walk right and experience yet another. Time contracts as you realize just how overwhelming your choices are. Gilded temple spires, gleaming shopping malls and ornate skyscrapers stand alongside tented noodle stands and blanket-on-the-pavement palm-readers. Night falls and huge glittering discotheques fashioned to resemble UFOs and Roman palaces vie with massage parlors drenched in red neon for the attention of the orbiting inhabitants of a city that never sleeps.

Whether native or newcomer, virtually every Bangkokian you meet has a story. Although no doubt a majority find themselves here owing to the simple fact that they were born in the city, a healthy percentage of the population hail from other parts of Thailand and from around

Page 5: Painted with ads, the Skytrain speeds along an elevated railway in central Bangkok.
Left: A spectacular view of Bangkok at night. The city's rapid development continues unabated, albeit tempered by a growing awareness of the need to balance the concrete jungle with natural greenery. This has led to the development of "pocket parks" in undeveloped parts of the city.

Illuminated temple buildings combine with light-festooned trees, a fading sunset and the blur of vehicle lights to produce one of Bangkok's classic dusk scenes.

The Victory Monument, commemorating the end of World War II, is one of the city's most immediately recognizable landmarks.

the world. Some migrate for the promise of work, others for the promise of a life in new and exciting circumstances.

Official estimates place Bangkok's population at eight million, though some sources claim this figure may be a million or two short. An astonishing 3,600 residents compete for every square kilometer, propelling a creative turbine that never ceases as the city's past and future co-evolve, from farms to freeways, spirit shrines to art galleries. Visitors may not be surprised to hear that one out of 10 Thai citizens lives in Bangkok, or that roughly 60% of the country's wealth is concentrated here.

Only a little over half of the city's inhabitants are in fact true Bangkok Thais, that is people born of Thai parentage who speak Bangkok Thai as their first language. Thais are found in all walks of life, although they make up the backbone of the city's blue-collar work force, prominently construction, automotive repair and river transport. Although Thais can naturally be found in all corners of the city, the old rich tend to live in walled manors in Suan Phlu and Pathumwan, the middle class in tall condo projects off Sukhumvit Road, the working class along the river and the poor in the slums of Khlong Toey or Makkasan.

Over a quarter of the city's population come from Chinese or mixed Thai and Chinese descent. Chinese influence can be felt throughout Central Thailand's Chao Phraya Delta but

Left: A stairway leading from the Skytrain platform at Siam Square leads to MBK Center, one of the most popular budget shopping centers in the city.
Right: Buses and cars edge along a city street during rush hour. Bangkok is notorious for its traffic jams and the opening of a new subway system in 2004 has helped alleviate the problem.

in Bangkok it is so strong that in certain areas of the city—such as Yaowarat, Bangkok's Chinatown, or Pathumwan, the city's wealthiest precinct—you can almost imagine you're in Hong Kong or Singapore rather than Thailand. The influence extends to the Bangkok dialect, which brims with Chinese vocabulary, even among non-Chinese. Many Chinese Thais in the capital can converse in at least one dialect from the old country, such as Cantonese, Hainanese, Hokkien or Chiu Chau, in addition to Thai.

Whether immigrant or Thailand-born, Chinese residents probably enjoy better relations with the majority population here than in any other country in Southeast Asia. Thai rulers in the 18th and 19th centuries made liberal use of Chinese businesspeople to infiltrate European trading houses, a move that helped defeat the colonial designs of the Europeans. The Thai monarchy also accepted the daughters of rich Chinese families into the royal court as consorts, thus deepening political connections and adding a Chinese bloodline that extends to the current Thai king.

Although Chinese Thais live in virtually every quarter of the sprawling city, their presence is most evident in a dense-ly populated core of multi-story shophouses along Charoen Krung and Yaowarat roads near the Chao Phraya River, a precinct known as Yaowarat or Sampeng. The Chinese in these areas tend to engage themselves in all manner of com-

Left: At the Lak Muang or City Pillar shrine, Bangkokians kneel and pay their respects to the capital's invisible guardian deities, while a hired Thai dance troupe offers a ceremonial performance.
Right: A *khon* (Thai classical dance-drama) troupe performs a chapter of the Indian epic Ramayana outdoors.

merce, from wholesale trade in auto parts to the manufacture of high-end kitchen utensils. In other parts of the city they dominate higher education, international trade, banking and white-collar employment in general.

Also prominent are people of South Asian descent, who make up Bangkok's second largest Asian minority. Most trace their heritage to northern India, including many Sikhs who immigrated after the 1947 Partition of India. Other South Asian nationalities found in Bangkok include Sinhalese, Bangladeshis, Nepalese and Pakistanis. Most of the city's South Asians can be found in two areas. The heaviest concentration find themselves wedged in at the north end of Yaowarat between Chakraphet and Phahurat roads, in an area known as Phahurat or Little India. South Asian residents are also more thinly spread along and nearby Charoen Krung Road, near the junctions with Silom and Surawong roads, an area collectively known as Bang Rak. In both areas they operate a multitude of successful retail businesses, particularly textile dealers and tailor shops.

Malays and Thais who are part-Malay and who adhere to Islam make up the third largest minority in Bangkok. Like residents of South Asian descent, many can be found living in Bang Rak, and like the majority Thais they tend to be found in blue-collar jobs.

Centuries before Thais migrated into the area, the Chao Phraya River delta in and around Bangkok was home to the

Left: With the Skytrain whizzing by above, city residents offer flowers, candles and incense to the most famous Brahma shrine in the capital.

Mon. Bangkokians of Mon descent can still be found in some districts, particularly on Ko Kret, an island in the middle of the river in northern Bangkok and in neighboring Pathum Thani Province. The Mon have their own language and culture, both of which have exercised a significant influence on modern Thai culture. The practice of Buddhism in Thailand in particular owes much to early Mon forms of Theravada Buddhism existent before and during the reign of King Rama IV, who incorporated certain religious reforms keyed to Mon Buddhism. Thai cuisine has also been influenced by Mon cooking, producing such dishes as *khao chae* (moist chilled rice served with sweetmeats, a hot season specialty).

Bangkok residents of European descent may number around 25,000. The vast majority, unlike their Asian counterparts, find themselves in Thailand for only a few months or years to work or study. Perhaps reflecting their significant roles in the early development of Bangkok, residents of German and British descent appear to be most prominent.

Yet the city continues to lure rural Thais, international investors, and curious visitors from around the world with its capacity to pull together the carnal, the spiritual and the entrepreneurial under one roof. Bangkok's legendary tolerance lends equal support to the monk and the playboy, to the beggar and the Benz dealer. You can slurp down a chili-laden plate of *phat khee mao* (fried rice noodles) from a street vendor while standing outside a US$250-a-night hotel. Bid your life savings on local shares at the Stock Exchange of Thailand or have your muscles gently kneaded for an hour and a half at a Thai massage hall for less than the price of a cinema ticket

Sleek high-rise towers, an elevated railway and traffic-lined avenues shape a typical cityscape.

in most world capitals. For absolutely free, take a meditation cell at Wat Mahathat and contemplate your life's choices for days, weeks or the rest of your life.

As varied as it is vast, Bangkok offers residents and visitors alike the assurance they will never be bored. One can move across the city on water via 18th-century canals, in the air aboard the sleek Skytrain or below ground in the high-tech Metropolitan Rapid Transit Authority (MRTA) subway. When hunger beckons, residents are spoiled by a panoply of the finest Thai restaurants anywhere in the kingdom, along with a host of other Asian cuisines—Chinese, Japanese, Korean, Burmese, Malay, Sri Lankan and Indian to name a few—and a broad range of European fare prepared by native chefs. Night falls and one can attend a classical Thai masked

The throne room in the Dusit Hall of the Grand Palace was used for royal receptions during the late 19th and early 20th centuries. Today the Thai king and queen reside at the newer Chitlada Palace, and the Grand Palace is used only on ceremonial occasions such as Coronation Day.

Above: This ornate dais at the Grand Palace was reserved for King Bhumibol Adulyadej during a short period when His Majesty ordained as a monk.
Right: Designed by British architects and built in 1882, the Phra Borom Maharatchawong or Grand Palace exhibits a blend of Thai and European styles.

dance-drama performance followed by a disco jaunt to hear a visiting DJ spin the latest house music.

In the midst of the ménage of international influences and epoch-leaping technologies, Bangkok never loses sight of its essential *khwaam pen thai* or "Thai-ness." Outside the tallest skyscrapers, office employees stop to offer flowers, incense and prayers to roofed spirit shrines, diminutive echoes from the past. Wheeled carts at curbside offer Thai herbal remedies and Buddhist amulets alongside espressos and Nintendo game cartridges. As the famed travel writer Pico Ayer, himself the cultural offspring of three continents, has noted about Bangkok, it is a city that is "immutably and ineffably itself."

Left: Two monumental wings of the Shangri-La overlook the Chao Phraya River at night

HISTORIC BANGKOK

Situated at the mouth of the kingdom's greatest river, and surrounded by the world's largest rice-producing cache, Bangkok serves as Thailand's nerve center, the quintessential primate city where the vast bulk of the country's wealth is concentrated.

That wealth, as well as the city's political and cultural identity, originally took shape 86 kilometers (53 miles) upriver in Ayuthaya, which served as the royal capital of Siam—as Thailand was then known—from 1350 to 1767. Encircled by rivers with access to the Gulf of Thailand, Ayuthaya flourished as a seaport courted by Dutch, Portuguese, French, English, Chinese and Japanese merchants. By the end of the 17th century the city's population had reached one million and Ayuthaya had become one of the wealthiest and most powerful cities in Asia. Virtually all foreign visitors claimed it to be the most illustrious city they had ever seen, beside which London and Paris paled in comparison.

"Among the Asian nations," wrote London visitor Engelbert Campfer, "the Kingdom of Siam is the greatest. The magnificence of the Ayuthaya Court is incomparable."

Throughout four centuries of Ayuthaya reign, several European powers tried without success to establish colonial relationships with the kingdom of Siam. An Asian power finally subdued the capital when the Burmese attacked in 1765, destroying most of Ayuthaya's Buddhist temples and royal edifices. Many Siamese were marched to Pegu, where they were forced to serve the Burmese court.

Four years after this devastating defeat at the hands of the Burmese, the Siamese regrouped under Phaya Taksin, a half-Chinese, half-Thai general who decided to move the capital farther south along the Chao Phraya River, closer to the Gulf of Siam. Thonburi Si Mahasamut, founded two hundred years earlier by a group of wealthy Thais who had turned it into an important trade entrepôt during the height of Ayuthaya's power, was a logical choice.

Fearing Thonburi was vulnerable to Burmese attack from the west, in 1782 Taksin's successor Phaya Chakri moved the capital across the river to a smaller settlement known as Bang Makok (Olive Plum Riverbank), named after the trees which grew there in abundance. As the first monarch of the new Chakri royal dynasty—which continues to this day—Phaya Chakri was later dubbed King Rama I.

Page 21: Thais gather at Wat Rajapradit to celebrate the Loi Krathong festival. Wat Rajapradit was founded in 1864.
Left: This 15th-century stupa (*chedi* in Thai), a depository for sacred Buddhist objects, typifies of the Ayuthaya style with its elongated, ribbed spire and slender reliquary dome.

Under Rama I, the Siamese erected a new royal palace, raised 10 kilometers (6 miles) of city walls and dug a system of canals to create a moated, royal 'island' known as Ko Ratanakosin. Sections of the 4.5-meter (15-foot) thick walls can still be seen near Wat Saket and the Golden Mount, and along the Chao Phraya River. The canal-moats still flow, albeit sluggishly, around the original royal district.

Master craftsmen who had survived the sacking of Ayuthaya designed and built several magnificent temples and royal administrative buildings for the new capital. In 1785, at a three-day consecration ceremony attended by tens of thousands of Siamese, the city was given a new name:

Krungthep mahanakhon bowon ratanakosin mahintara ayuthaya mahadilok popnopparat ratchathani burirom udomratchaniwet mahasathan amonpima avatansathir sakkathatitya visnukamprasit.

This lexical feat translates roughly as "Great city of angels, the repository of divine gems, the great land unconquerable, the grand and prominent realm, the royal and delightful capital city full of nine noble gems, the highest royal dwelling and grand palace, the divine shelter and living place of reincarnated spirits." Foreign traders continued to call the capital Bang Makok, which eventually truncated itself to "Bangkok," the name most commonly known to the outside world today.

Top right: Stupas pierce the sunset at 14th-century Wat Si Sanphet, the largest temple complex at the former royal capital of Ayuthaya.
Bottom right: The ruins at Wat Ratburana are famous for their large corncob-shaped stupas influenced by temple architecture at Angkor.

Opposite, top left to right: Ayuthaya-era Buddhist art reveled in the use of crowns and other regalia, as found on this relief sculpture of Avalokitesvara, the compassionate and world-preserving Buddha-to-be; Many Brahmanist deities found their way into Ayuthaya's religious art following the Thai conquest of Angkor, including this bronze sculpture of Vishnu, now in a collection at the National Museum; Brahma, the four-faced Hindu creator god, has remained a popular sacred art subject throughout most of Thai history.

Opposite, bottom left to right: Khmer-style sandstone Buddhas, such as this one displaying exquisite facial features, represent the pinnacle of Thai art during the Lopburi era; Hailing from between the 6th to 10th century AD, this *dhammachakka* or wheel of natural law was the most popular Buddhist symbol in Thailand's Dvaravati kingdom; This bronze Mahayana Buddhist bodhisattva (saint or Buddha-to-be) was found in southern Thailand and is considered to be one of the most important works of the Srivijaya empire.

Left: Representing courage, strength and steadfastness, the elephant has long been one of Thailand's most important national symbols. In this sculpture a royal attendant makes an offering to an unseen monarch.

The Thais, meanwhile, commonly use a shortened version of the name, Krung Thep (City of Angels) or, when referring to the city and burgeoning metropolitan area surrounding it, Krung Thep Mahanakhon (Metropolis of the City of Angels).

Under the reigns of kings Rama II and Rama III, more temples were built and the system of rivers, streams and natural canals surrounding the capital was augmented by the excavation of additional waterways. Waterborne traffic dominated the city, supplemented by a meager network of footpaths, well into the middle of the 19th century.

In response to requests from diplomats and international merchants, Rama IV (King Mongkut, 1851–1868) established a handful of roadways suitable for horse-drawn carriages and rickshaws in the mid-1800s. The first—and most ambitious road project for nearly a century to come—was Charoen Krung Road (also known by its English name, New Road), which ran 10 kilometers (6 miles) south from Wat Pho along the east bank of the Chao Phraya River. This swathe of hand-laid cobblestone, which took four years to finish, eventually accommodated a tramway as well as early automobiles.

Rama IV also ordered the construction of the much shorter Bamrung Meuang and Feuang Nakhon roads to provide access to royal temples from Charoen Krung. His successor Rama V (King Chulalongkorn, 1868–1910) added the much wider Ratchadamnoen Klang Road to provide a suitably royal promenade—modeled after the Champs Elysées and lined with ornamental gardens—situated between the Grand Palace and the expanding commercial center to the east of Ko Ratanakosin.

Opposite: Wat Pho, the oldest monastery in Bangkok, as it appeared in the late 19th century.

By this time Bangkok's city limits encompassed no more than a dozen square kilometers (4.5 square miles). Despite its modest size, the capital administered the much larger kingdom of Siam—which extended well into parts of what are today Laos, Cambodia and Malaysia—quite well. Even more impressive, Siamese rulers were able to stave off steady and at times intense pressure from the Portuguese, the Dutch, the French and the English, all of whom at one time or another harbored desires to add Siam to their colonial portfolios. By the end of the 19th century, France and England had established imperial rule in every one of Siam's neighboring countries—the French in Indochina and the English in Burma and Malaya.

Was it a simple historical accident that Siam became the only South or Southeast Asian country never to be ruled by a foreign power? Or was the structure of Thai society itself is responsible for resisting European colonialization? Whatever the reason, Bangkok's ability to maintain Siam's independence meant that the kingdom was free to draw upon the talents of any architect or transport developer in the world, a freedom that helps explain the enormous variety—planned and unplanned—in the capital today.

Germans were hired to design and build railways emanating from the capital, while the Dutch contributed Bangkok's central railway station, today considered a minor masterpiece of civic Art Deco. Italian sculptor Corrado Feroci contributed the four-winged Democracy Monument and other mementoes of national pride to the city and helped found the country's first fine arts university. Americans

Above: These lushly painted temple doors, depicting figures from the Ramayana, show a blend of Thai and Chinese influence.
Right: A mural scene inside the cloisters of Wat Phra Kaew, originally painted in the late 18th century, depict Wat Phra Kaew itself along with other Bangkok architecture of that era.

established Siam's first printing press along with the kingdom's first newspaper.

As the 20th century roared across Asia, fueled by a burst of creativity Siam had never seen before, Bangkok grew from a mere 13 square kilometers (5 square miles) in 1900 to an astounding metropolitan area of over 330 square kilometers (127 square miles) by the century's end. Today Krung Thep Mahanakhon encompasses Bangkok and the former capital of Thonburi, across the Chao Phraya River to the west, along with the densely populated provinces of Samut Prakan to the east and Nonthaburi to the north.

Today Bangkok groans under the weight of an overburdened infrastructure. Road surfaces, occupying among the world's lowest percentages relative to the overall city plan for a city of this size, remain insufficient for the number of Bangkok-registered cars, yet up to a thousand new vehicles climb onto the streets everyday. Yet the city continues to lure rural Thais, international investors, and curious visitors from around the world with its capacity to pull together the carnal, the spiritual and the entrepreneurial under one roof.

Page 30: One of the earliest known photographs of a public Thai classical dance performance.

Page 31: Built in the mid-1800s, Charoen Krung Road paralleled the Chao Phraya River and was originally meant for horse carriages and rickshaws. A tramway was added later, and today it is one of the busiest streets in Bangkok.

Left: By the 19th century Bangkok was an important port of call for trading ships from Europe, America, China and the Dutch East Indies.

"There was a rich, dim light in the room, which was cool and wainscoted entirely with dark red wood, and there was only one long, low window, with turned bars of the same wood... Richness and harmony characterised the room, and it was distinctively Malay, one could not say that it reminded one of anything except of the flecked and coloured light which streams through dark, old, stained glass."
— Isabella L. Bird, *The Golden Chersonese and the Way Thither* (1883)

THE VENICE
OF THE EAST

One of the quickest ways to neutralize Bangkok's metropolitan overload is to leave the concrete behind and disappear into Bangkok's network of canals and rivers. Criss-crossing the city in all directions, these murky green waterways move cargo and passenger traffic both within the city and without, provide a seemingly endless source of water for bathing, cooking, irrigation and recreation, and conjure up a parallel universe in which 18th-century Siam collides with 21st-century Thailand. Viewed from above, Bangkok's canal world resembles a quirky, skewed mandala, the quasi-circular diagrams created by Buddhist artists as an object for meditation. Much like Hindu-Buddhist mythology's Mount Meru, around which the cosmos unfolds in concentric continents alternating with slender cosmic oceans, Thailand's sweltering capital straddles a spider web of natural and artificial canals fanning out through sultry river delta for several hundred square miles.

Royal State Barge, Siam.

The Thais have always had a deep affinity for water, dating to the first millennium when they began migrating into river valleys throughout Thailand and Laos and Myanmar.

Buckminster Fuller believed the prevalence of the Meru myth in South and Southeast Asia suggested a migration from the Indian and Pacific ocean archipelagos and continental coasts to the Himalayan heart of Asia. For Fuller the orderly alternation of land and water in the Meru mandala pointed to an oceanic origin for Asian civilization and religious archetypes.

Whatever the circumstances, the Siamese never strayed far from water. Thailand's ruling monarchy, which has flourished for nearly a thousand years, transferred the royal capital from central Thailand's Ayuthaya—itself surrounded by canals and rivers—to the banks of the Chao Phraya River in 1769 following a disastrous war with the Burmese.

Using thousands of Khmer prisoners of war, King Rama I augmented Bangkok's natural canal-and-river system by adding hundreds of artificial waterways. All of these fed into Thailand's vital hydraulic lifeline, the broad Chao Phraya River, which bisected the city center into two halves, Bangkok proper and Thonburi, the river's right bank. The

Page 35: A speedboat ferries passengers along one of Bangkok's many *khlongs* or canals. For much of the late 20th century, *khlongs* were especially important for people wanting to beat the traffic congestion on Bangkok's crowded streets.
Left top: Royal elephant receives a ritual washing in the late 19th century.
Left bottom: The king's royal barge, carved from a single teak trunk and crewed by 50 oarsmen, has been in use since the turn of the 19th century for ceremonial occasions on the Chao Phraya River.
Right: At one time most Bangkokians lived in simple wood-and-bamboo houseboats moored along the city's rivers and canals.

Siam Bangkok.

Chao Phraya in turn disgorges itself into the Gulf of Thailand, a vast cul-de-sac of the South China Sea.

The canal expansion changed the geography of the city. Taking one of the river's largest natural curves, city planners added two lengthy canals, Banglamphu Canal and Ong Ang Canal, to create a royal island known as Ko Ratanakosin. Ko Ratanakosin quickly accumulated an impressive architectural portfolio centered around the Grand Palace, political hub of the new Siamese capital.

In 1782, Brahman priests and Buddhist monks consecrated the palace together with an adjacent royal monastery, Wat Phra Kaew, now considered the holiest of Thailand's *wats*. Lining the long, shaded cloisters of this stunning monastery (also known as the Temple of the Emerald Buddha), deep-hued frescoes, highlighted with rich golds and watery blues, transpose the Hindu god Rama's heroic exploits onto visions of Bangkok's canal network 200 years ago.

Portuguese priest Fernao Mendez Pinto was the first to use the epithet "Venice of the East," referring not to Bangkok but to Ayuthaya, in a letter to the Society of Jesus in Lisbon in 1554, but two hundred years later the term came to be used to describe the new Bangkok capital as well. In 1855, British envoy Sir John Bowring noted in his reports: "The highways of Bangkok are not streets or roads but the river and the canals. Boats are the universal means of conveyance and communication."

Floating markets have been a feature of waterborne culture surrounding Bangkok for several centuries.

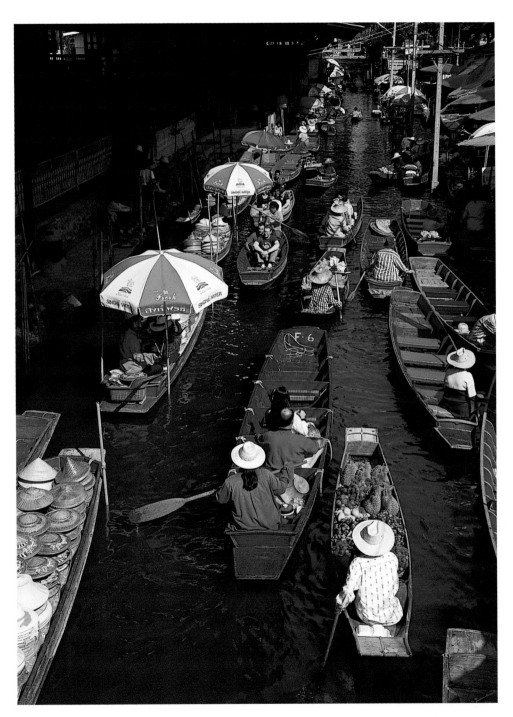

On the eve of the coronation of King Rama VI in 1911, a young Italian nobleman named Salvatore Besso wrote:

The Venice of the Far East—the capital still wrapped in mystery, in spite of the thousand efforts of modernism amid its maze of canals, and in spite of the popularity of the reigning monarch… from the crowded dock-roads of the River which reminds one of the Giudecca, across the intricate mass of the Chinese quarter which, whilst resembling Canton, is still more Venetian. Were it not for the queues, almond eyes and odors, decided-ly Oriental, the illusion would very often be com-plete… the European residences and sporting clubs shady and surrounded by canals which reminded me of [Venice]… the canals ploughed by sampans, which the rowers guide standing as in Venice… little bridges and tiny gardens, reflecting in the quiet water the drooping foliage of ancient trees as in the remotest corners of the City of the Doges. The Royal Quarter, rich in parks, temples and palaces all a dazzling vari-ety of color and cadences, which give one the impres-sion of being in Venice, a wild and primitive Venice.

Visiting traders and diplomats from Europe marveled not only at the sheer size of the waterways but also the exotic life

Left: Boat vendors purvey their wares on Khlong Damnoen Saduak.
Right: Monks gaze at the main stupa at Wat Arun from the inside of a bus-like boat service that runs daily along the Chao Phraya River, making stops along both banks every few hundred meters.

Left: Vendors in rowed skiffs chat while waiting for customers at the main floating market in Damnoen Saduak.

Above: This lampshade-shaped hat is typical headwear for farmers in central Thailand.

Opposite top: Freshwater fish harvested in canals, rivers and lakes on the outskirts of Bangkok are sold from plastic tubs on a teak pier.

Opposite bottom: Houses and shops built on stilted piers have long replaced floating houseboats along Bangkok's rivers and canals.

encountered both on and off the water. While walking along the banks of the Chao Phraya one afternoon in 1824, English trader Robert Hunter spotted what he thought was a creature with eight limbs and two heads swimming in the river. When the oddity lifted itself onto a canoe, Hunter was surprised to see it was in fact two 13-year-old boys who were fused together at the chest. The Briton was so intrigued that he sponsored a medical examination of the boys and later introduced them to Bangkok's Western social circuits as "The Siamese Twins."

Throughout the history of the Chakri Dynasty, royal administrations added to the system. Khlong Mahawawat (*khlong* means "canal") was dug during the reign of King Rama IV to link the Chao Phraya River with the Tha Chin River. Lined with fruit orchards and stilted houses draped with fishing nets, Khlong Mahawawat is still one of the most traditional and least visited of the Bangkok canals. Khlong Saen Saep came about to shorten travel between the Chao Phraya and Bang Pakong rivers, and today is heavily used by boat taxi commuters moving across the city from east to west and vice versa. Likewise both the Khlong Sunak Hon and Khlong Damnoen Saduak connect the Tha Chin and Mae Klong rivers.

The section of the Chao Phraya River extending between the Bangkok Noi and Bangkok Yai canals was originally itself a canal dug as a shortcut across a large loop in the original river course. This canal broadened and merged with the Chao Phraya River such that today most people assume it's the natural course of the river. Meanwhile the original river

loop narrowed and became shallower, becoming the Bangkok Noi and Bangkok Yai "canals."

Following World War II, when the Japanese briefly occupied parts of the city, Thai engineers built bridges over the Chao Phraya River and began filling in canals to provide space for new roads and shophouses. Although many residents continued to occupy stilted houses along the *khlong* and to move about their neighborhoods by boat, a future of automobiles and asphalt appeared inevitable.

However as Bangkok tumbled headlong into the 1980s, racking up double-digit growth for over a decade, gridlock traffic and choking vehicle fumes induced nostalgia for the city's waterborne origins. Bangkokians stopped filling in the canals and restored water taxi routes that had lapsed during the boom years.

Today the city's waterways carry a fleet of diverse watercraft. Crowded water taxis weave among longtail boats, named for the three-meter (10-foot) propeller shafts jutting from the stern and mounted on gimbals for simple steering. Ancient teak ferries used for short river trips and huge iron barges heaped with gravel or rice and chained together to create barge trains also ply the waterways. Along their banks, homes, trading houses and temples remain oriented towards water life and provide a fascinating glimpse into a past when Thais still considered themselves *jao nam* or "water lords."

Gliding west off the Chao Phraya into Khlong Bangkok Noi knocks 50 years off big city progress. As the boat penetrates Bangkok's right bank, the scenery transforms into a snug corridor of teak houses on stilts, old Buddhist temples

and banana groves. Thai women in straw lampshade hats hawk steaming bowls of rice noodles from wooden canoes. Mobile banks and post offices putter along atop tiny barges, further demonstrating that virtually any errand one might accomplish on land can also be done on water.

From Bangkok Noi, public boats continue up Khlong Om, lined by plantations growing the spiky, strong-smelling durian. Another turn in the maze links up with Khlong Mon and one whooshes past gold-spired temples, old wooden piers and hothouses filled with exotic orchids.

Authentic floating markets, or *talat nam*, in which wooden canoes laden with fruits, vegetables, noodles and handicrafts cluster together near bridges and riverbanks waiting for customers, have disappeared from central Bangkok. Adjacent Samut Songkhram Province, however, practically floats on canals intersecting the lazy bends of the Mae Klong River, creating the perfect environment for *talat nam*. Some floating markets convene only during certain moon phases of the lunar calendar. For example, the Bang Noi Floating Market takes place in nearby Bang Noi on the third, eighth and 13th days of both the waxing and waning moons, while the Kha Pier Floating Market meets on the second, seventh and 12th days of the waxing and waning moons. Any Thai calendar, available for a few baht in a market, can show you which days of the solar month coincide with this lunar schedule.

The longer one lingers on Bangkok's waters, the closer one gets to "Thai-ness", so much so that it could be said that until you've skimmed the choppy canals of the great city, you haven't really arrived in Thailand.

Right: A colorful longtail boat skims across the Chao Phraya River in front of the Oriental Hotel.

ROYAL AND RELIGIOUS SIGHTS

"Here and there in the distance... towered great piles of masonry, king's palaces, temples, gorgeous and dilapidated, crumbling under the vertical sunlight, tremendous, overpowering, almost palpable, which seemed to enter one's breast with the breath of one's nostrils and soak into one's ribs through every pore of one's skin."

– Joseph Conrad

When Bangkok became the capital of the kingdom of Siam in 1782, the first task set before the new city planners was to create hallowed ground for royal palaces and Buddhist monasteries. Indian astrologers and high-ranking Buddhist monks conferred to select and consecrate the most auspicious riverside locations, marking them off with small carved stone pillars. Siam's most talented architects and artisans then weighed in, creating majestic and ornate edifices designed to astound all who ventured into the new capital.

The original temples and palaces along the Chao Phraya riverbanks continue to make a lasting impression on new arrivals. Whether approaching by river or by road, from a distance one's eye immediately catches the sunlight refracting off the multitude of gilded spires peeking out over the immense walls of Wat Phra Kaew, the "Temple of the Emerald Buddha." Inside the brick-and-stucco walls, one can easily lose oneself amidst the vast grounds, which contain over a hundred buildings representing more than two centuries of royal history and architectural experimentation.

Inside the tallest and most ornate of the temple buildings, roofed with gleaming orange and green tiles and supported by pillars encrusted with bright blue mosaics and gilded, carved plaster, sits the kingdom's holiest Buddha image. Leaving their shoes at the chapel entrance, tourists and residents alike sit on the floor before the diminutive Buddha—perched atop a high pedestal overlooking the ebb and flow of visiting worshippers—soaking up the atmosphere of silent awe and veneration. The significance of this image extends beyond Thai Buddhism to encompass Thai nationalism and sovereignty, and thus even Thais of non-Buddhist backgrounds offer their respects.

In the cloister adjacent to this chapel on the grounds of Wat Phra Kaew, deeply hued 18th-century murals bring to life the Ramakian, the Thai version of the Indian Ramayana epic. Those who care to follow all 178 panels begin their journey at the north gate and then move clockwise around the compound. On the other side of the Emerald Buddha chapel, the fantasy continues with the Grand Palace, a collection of two- and three-story buildings that fuse Italian Renaissance and traditional Thai architecture. Although the Thai royal family no longer lives here, having moved to Chitlada Palace

Page 46: Boat figureheads are believed to help protect the boat from misfortune and are also a symbol of authority. This seven-headed figurehead is found on several of Bangkok's royal barges.
Page 47: The large statue of the Reclining Buddha in Wat Pho represents the position adopted by Buddha before his death.
Left: An open-air shrine inside the Wat Phra Kaew compound is thronged with worshippers.
Right: The carefully tended gardens surrounding the Grand Palace offer a welcome respite from Bangkok's concrete and asphalt.

Above: Fireworks burst over an illuminated Grand Palace and Wat Phra Kaew.
Right: The main *prasat* (four-portico chapel) at Wat Phra Kaew gleams in the light of dusk.

elsewhere in the city in the early 20th century, the structures are still treated with much reverence and may be admired from the outside only. The Chakri Mahaprasat, erected in 1882 by British architects, stands out as the largest and most ornate, with three connected wings, each topped by a separate tiered spire. Because the spires resemble the highly ornate *chada* or Thai classical dancer's headdress, Thais often whimsically refer to the building as *farang sai chada* (European wearing a *chada*).

Honing in on a second set of tall stupa spires poking out from another walled compound nearby, one is pulled towards Wat Pho (Wat Phra Chetuphon) a couple of hundred meters away. Enter the old heavy wooden gates and you'll immediately breathe in the air of antiquity, borne from the fact that this is the oldest royal *wat* in Bangkok, and one that hasn't been renovated as many times or as lavishly as Wat Phra Kaew.

Occupying a temple site dating to the 16th century, Wat Pho was renovated in 1782, when a huge hall was raised in order to enclose the world's longest reclining Buddha. Standing beneath the 46-meter (150-foot) long, 15-meter (50-foot) high image, fashioned from delicately carved plaster finished in gold leaf and smoothed around a brick core, one can't help but sense the dedication to their religion the Thais who created this image must have felt.

Left: Stupas at Wat Arun (often called the Temple of the Dawn in English) are studded with broken pieces of colorful Chinese porcelain. In the 19th century, when Wat Arun was built, old porcelain plates and cups arrived in Thailand as ballast in the holds of cargo ships from China.
Right: Smaller decorated stupas dot the grounds at Wat Phra Kaew.

Above, left to right: A Thai man has his head shaved in preparation for ordination as a Buddhist monk; Wat Pho contains many old and venerable Buddha images, including this one sheltered by a nine-tiered umbrella, a symbol of royalty; This Buddha at Wat Pho sits on a coiled, multi-headed *naga*, a mythical water serpent associated with the protection and preservation of Buddhism.

Although many visitors never make it beyond Wat Pho's centerpiece, the reclining Buddha chapel, those who take the time to explore further will be rewarded by the sight of two particularly fine seated images, the Phra Jinnarat and Phra Jinachi, found in separate chapels elsewhere in the compound. Both hail from the Sukhothai era (13th–15th centuries), when Thai Buddhist sculpture reached its artistic zenith, as exemplified by the boneless, slightly pneumatic grace of the fingers, hands, arms and legs—symbolic of perfect peace attained through meditation. Continue eastward in the compound to bask in the symmetry of no fewer than 394 identical gilded Buddhas, each of them slightly larger than life-size, lining a cloistered quadrangle.

Those who would like to see at least one royal *wat* that few tourists visit, yet is comparable to Wat Pho or Wat Phra Kaew in the level of artistic achievement, would do well to seek out Wat Tritosathep Mahawarawihan in the Banglamphu district. Here Chakrabhand Pasayakrit's post-modern Buddhist murals, glowing with deep, jewel-like colors, are being hailed as a masterwork of Thai Buddhist art of any era.

Although Bangkok boasts several other *wat* of royal pedigree, each of them impressive in its own right, perhaps more remarkable still is the sheer number of monasteries scattered around the city—over 300—all of them supporting the kingdom's most important cultural constant, Theravada Buddhism. Serving as both social and administrative center for the religion, the typical Bangkok *wat* usually consists of a walled compound containing several buildings constructed in the traditional Thai style with steep, swooping rooflines and colorful interior wall murals. Various shades of red, green, and orange make up the predominant color scheme. The most important structures will contain solemn Buddha statues that have been cast in bronze or carved from stone, wood or other materials.

Walk the streets of Bangkok early in the morning, and you'll catch the flash of shaved heads bobbing above bright ochre robes, as monks all over the city engage in *bindabaht*, the daily house-to-house alms-food gathering. Thai men are expected to shave their heads and don monastic robes temporarily at least once in their lives. Some enter the monkhood twice, first as 10-vow novices in their preteen years and again as fully ordained, 227-vow monks sometime after the age of 20. Monks depend on the faithful for their daily meals—permitted only

before noon and collected from lay devotees in large black-lacquered bowls.

Green onion domes looming over lower rooftops nearby belong to mosques and mark the immediate neighborhood as Muslim, while brightly painted cement spires may indicate the presence of a Hindu temple. Wander down congested Chakraphet Road in the Phahurat district to find Sri Gurusingh Sabha, a Sikh temple where visitors are very welcome. A handful of steepled Christian churches, including a few historic ones, can be found in the vicinity of the Chao Phraya River as well. In Chinatown, large round doorways topped with heavily inscribed Chinese characters

A monk catches up on daily news under the watchful gaze of a Chinese sentry at Wat Pho.

and flanked by red paper lanterns mark the location of *san jao,* temples dedicated to the worship of Buddhist, Taoist and Confucian deities.

Thai royal ceremony is almost exclusively the domain of one of the most ancient religious traditions still functioning within the kingdom, Brahmanism. White-robed, topknotted priests of Indian descent keep alive an arcane collection of rituals that, it is generally believed, must be performed at regular intervals to sustain the three pillars of Thai nationhood, namely sovereignty, religion and the monarchy. Most of these rituals are performed privately at a complex of shrines near Wat Suthat in the center of the city. Devasathan ("Abode of Gods") contains shrines to Shiva and Ganesha and thus hosts priestly ceremonies in the Shaiva tradition, while the smaller Sathan Phra Narai ("Abode of Vishnu") is reserved for Vaishnava ritual.

Left: Wat Benjamabophit boasts one of the few chapels in Bangkok laid out in a cruciform plan. **Above:** A trio of monks strolls across a canal running through their monastery compound.

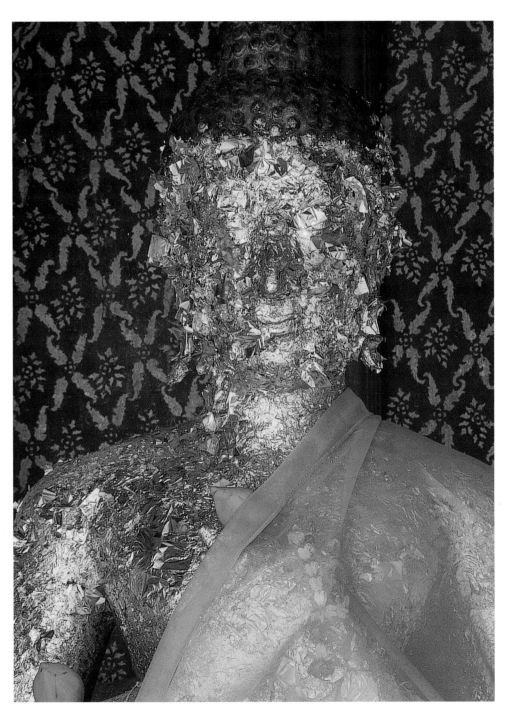

Animism predated the arrival of all other religions in Bangkok and still plays an important role in the everyday life of most city residents. Believing that *phra phum* or guardian spirits inhabit rivers, canals, trees, and other natural features, and that these spirits must be placated whenever humans trespass upon or make use of these features, the Thais build spirit shrines to house the displaced spirits. These dollhouse-like structures perch on wood or cement pillars next to their homes and receive daily offerings of rice, fruit, flowers and water. Peek inside one of these spirit homes and you'll typically see a collection of ceramic or plastic figurines representing the property's guardian spirits.

Larger and more elaborate spirit shrines stand alongside hotels and office buildings. In such cases it's popular to replace traditional Thai figurines with larger Indian deities. Originally built to ward off bad luck during the construction of the Erawan Hotel (torn down to make way for the Grand Hyatt Erawan years ago), the mosaic-encrusted pavilion next to the Grand Hyatt Erawan shelters a shining bronze representation of the four-headed deity Brahma, the Hindu God of Creation. At all times of the day you'll see Thais kneeling before Brahma with colorful offerings of flowers, incense and candles, praying for favors. Visit the incense-clouded Erawan Shrine around sunset and you'll enjoy the circumambulations of costumed Thai dancers, hired by supplicants who believe their prayers have been answered and accompanied by live Thai classic music.

Behind the Hilton Hotel, carved stone and wooden phalluses surround a shrine built by local millionaire Nai Loet to

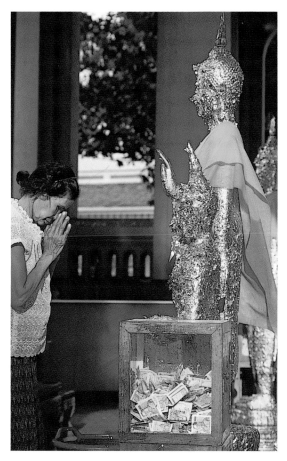

Left: The face and shoulder of this Buddha image is encrusted with goldleaf applied by worshippers.

Above: Worshippers donate a few baht to the temple in exchange for small squares of very thin goldleaf. They then press the gold squares onto Buddha images to show their appreciation and support of the Buddhist teachings.

This Wat Phra Kaew mural commemorates the coronation of King Rama I at the Grand Palace royal pavilion.

An intricate mural depicting palace life in 18th and early 19th-century Bangkok.

honor Mae Thap Thim, a female deity who resides in an old banyan tree on the site. A visit to this shrine, it is said, will fortify your chances for abundant progeny.

By far the most important spirit shrine in the city harbors Bangkok's guardian deity, Phra Sayam Thewathirat. Opposite the eastern wall of Wat Phra Kaew, this two-room, crowned pavilion shelters a 108-inch, gilded wooden pillar—the city standard or *lak meuang*—erected in 1782 during the founding of the new capital. Here the atmosphere of spirit worship is truly intoxicating, as Bangkokians stream in bearing pig heads and bottles of whiskey to offer the spirit as clouds of incense and jasmine swirl around the room, and the shrine musicians hammer away on their wooden xylophones and brass gongs. In return for this, it is believed, Phra Sayam Thewathirat looks after the city of 10 million inhabitants.

The Thais bestow certain Thai royal spirits with similar guardian qualities. The spirit of King Rama V, who ruled over Siam from 1868–1910 and who is particularly venerated for having successfully resisted colonialism, is thought to remain active in Bangkok today. Every Tuesday evening thousands of Bangkokians throng a bronze equestrian statue of Rama V opposite Abhisek Dusit Throne Hall, offering candles, pink roses, incense and liquor to the royal demigod.

If you see a yellow Rolls Royce flashing by with a police escort along the city's avenues, you've just caught a glimpse of Thailand's longest reigning monarch—indeed the longest-reigning living monarch anywhere in the world, King Bhumibol Adulyadej. Having ascended the throne in 1946, His Majesty administers royal duties from Chitlada Palace in

the city's Dusit precinct, north of Ko Ratanakosin. On Coronation Day and on his Royal Birthday the city is festooned with strings of lights and portraits of the King.

As protector of both nation and religion, His Majesty presides over several important Buddhist and Brahmanist ceremonies during the year. Among the more colorful of these are the seasonal robe-changing of the jade Buddha in Wat Phra Kaew and the annual Royal Ploughing Ceremony, in which ceremonial rice is sowed to insure a robust economy for the coming year, at Sanam Luang.

With the protection of the humblest of earth spirits to the most powerful royal persona in the nation, Bangkokians believe that the vigor and longevity of their city is assured.

Opposite: Royal barges, dug out from huge trunks of teak nearly 200 years ago, are brought out for processions along the Chao Phraya River.
Above: A parade of the royal guard takes place on Royal Plaza, in front of a former throne hall now used by the civilian government.
Next spread: Wat Phra Kaew boasts some of the most spectacular temple architecture in Thailand. It is home to the Emerald Buddha and is thronged by thousands of worshippers every day.

"In Bangkok at twelve o'clock they foam at the mouth and run,
But mad dogs and Englishmen go out in the midday sun."

Noel Coward

VISITING BANGKOK TODAY

Bangkok in the 21st century remains one of Southeast Asia's most intriguing and perpetually surprising cities. Double-digit economic growth during the last decades of the past century brought air-conditioned shopping malls, maple-and-chrome coffeeshops, world-class architectural monuments and many other accoutrements of civilization. Yet the city is as far from being 'tamed' by international ideas and technology as when it was founded over 200 years ago.

Early Bangkok was as much a citadel as a city. Today massive whitewashed walls punctured by tiny windows and topped with neat crenulations still loom over one end of trendy Phra Athit Road, thrusting out towards the Chao Phraya River. On the other side of the battlements, Banglamphu Canal cuts away from the river at a sharp angle, creating the northern tip of Ko Ratanakosin, the royal island that once was the whole of Bangkok. Although often neglected by residents and visitors alike, here stands Phra Sumen fort, one of the capital's pivotal points in understanding the city's original plan.

Erected in 1783, Phra Sumen fort is an octagonal, brick-and-stucco bunker. It was was one of 14 city fortresses built along Banglamphu Canal, which forms a bow-shaped arc carving an island out of the Chao Phraya River's left bank.

In the other direction, the seven-kilometer (four-mile) canal curves gently inland towards Mahakan Fort, marking the southern reach of Ko Ratanakosin. Of the four-meter (13-foot) high, three-meter (10-foot) thick ramparts that once lined the entire canal, only Phra Sumen and Mahakan have been preserved to remind us what 18th-century Bangkok really was about—keeping foreign armies at bay.

Disembark at the Chao Phraya River pier of Tha Tien today, weave your way through the vendor carts selling grilled squid and rice noodles, and you'll find yourself standing between two rows of shophouses of the sort once found along all the streets near the river. The deep, shaded porticoes of the ground floor, topped by upper stories displaying tall, shuttered windows and delicate plaster foliage preserve the elegance of old Bangkok's "grand Victorian ladies." Inside, the ground floors will display rich multi-colored tiles of French, Italian or Dutch design, while upper floors are planked with polished teak.

Page 66: An ornate roof detail from a building on Bangkok's National Museum compound.
Page 67: This reconstruction of a riverbank community is located in a large open air museum known as Muang Boran, or the Ancient City.
Left: Lumphini Park, named for the Buddha's birthplace in Nepal, is the city's largest and most popular park.
Right: Flanking a nearly forgotten canal, Sathon Road cuts through Bangkok's financial district and terminates at a bridge over the Chao Phraya River.

Above: Hawker stalls in the main tourist areas along Silom Road and Sukhumvit Road. display all manner of locally crafted yet inexpensive fashions perfect for casual holiday wear.

Above: Jewelry for sale in Bangkok runs the gamut from costume jewelry to rare hand-polished gems.
Right: Thailand is renowned for its sumptuous hand-woven silks, and Bangkok stocks the greatest selection in the kingdom.

Bangkok's oldest residential and business district fans out along the Chao Phraya River between Phra Pin Klao Bridge and Hualamphong station. One of the liveliest quarters of the capital, Bangkok's Chinatown encompasses a congested array of hardware, wholesale food, textiles, printing, automotive and gold shops, mixed in with apartment buildings, pawn-shops, Chinese temples, noodle-and-dim-sum cafes and the best Chinese banquet houses in the city.

In the 19th century, Victorian influences from Great Britain combined with Thai vernacular architecture to pro-duce many of the capital's most attractive royal villas. The most impressive of them all, Vimanmek Mansion, served as a palace for King Rama V and is the largest teak structure in the world.

Fully realized examples of Thai Deco from the 1920s and 1930s can be found along Chinatown's main streets, particu-larly Yaowarat Road. Whimsical Thai Deco-style sculptures—the Eiffel Tower, a lion, an elephant, a Moorish dome—sur-mount vertical towers over the main doorways. Other sur-viving examples include the Chalermkrung Royal Theatre, the Royal Hotel, Ratchadamnoen Boxing Stadium and the Bangkok general post office.

Towards the southwestern edge of Chinatown, where Padung Krung Kasem Canal feeds back into the Chao Phraya River, a Chinese entrepreneur named Chao Sua Son built a small market named Talat Noi where larger riverboats could offload wholesale goods to Chinatown merchants. Talat Noi serves as a cultural and geographic bridge between the pre-dominantly Chinese ambience of Yaowarat Chinatown to

Clockwise from top left: Thai celadon, hand-thrown pottery with a green-gray glaze invented in northern Thailand, is one of Bangkok's best buys; Buddha statues, figurines and miniature reliefs are a favorite Bangkok purchase; For skill and value, Bangkok's gem-cutters have no equal in Asia. Although some gemstones are locally mined, most come from Cambodia, Myanmar and Sri Lanka but are cut and polished in Bangkok.; *Benjarong* or five-color ceramics were originally made in China for the royal Thai market in the 19th century, but have long since become a local product cherished by Thais and foreigners alike.

Clockwise from top left: Most silverwork hails from Chiang Mai, where artisans practice a silversmithing tradition dating back several centuries; Hand-woven Thai fabrics, whether silk or cotton, tend to be very sturdy and thus make excellent pillow covers; These cane-woven baskets, with flared wooden footing, were originally designed to hold Thai sticky rice. Many visitors take them home to use for decoration or for storing things around the house; Bangkok's central district abounds with shops selling all manner of arts and antiques.

the immediate north and the almost exclusively Western–historically speaking–district of European trading houses and embassies to the immediate south.

South of Talat Noi at least two or more miles of the Chao Phraya riverside was once given over to such international mercantile enterprises as the East Asiatic Co, Chartered Bank, British Dispensary, Bombay Burmah Trading Co, Banque de l'Indochine, Messrs Howarth Erskine, as well as the French, Portuguese, Russian, British, American, German and Italian embassies. For the era, the well-financed architecture for this area–known as Bang Rak–was Bangkok's most flamboyant, a mixture of grand neo-classical fronts, shuttered Victorian windows and Beaux Arts ornamentation. Many of these old buildings have survived to the present, including the venerable Oriental Hotel, the city's oldest hostelry. Many of these historic buildings have been obscured by more modern structures along Charoen Krung Road, and the best way to appreciate them as a group is from the river itself, by boat.

To the north, wedged between Chinatown and Phra Pin Klao, is a relatively small but densely populated district called Phahurat, center for all things Indian in Bangkok. In the district's culinary heart, Chakraphet Road swoons in the heady aroma of Indian spices, strong tea and rose-scented sweets. At one time immigrants from India wielded almost total control over Bangkok's textile market, and Phahurat's

Left: An elderly European couple pause for cold beer at a streetside bar along Sukhumvit Road.
Right: On the bustling streets of Bangkok there's always room for a few tables of T-shirts and sunglasses for the tourists.

Clockwise from top left: Street markets like this one provide some of the best eating in Bangkok; Seafood lovers will find fresh offerings from the Gulf of Thailand and Andaman Sea close at hand almost anywhere in the city; City residents convene for cold drinks and bowls of noodles at every opportunity; Satay—chunks of marinated meat grilled on bamboo skewers—are a very common street food.

Clockwise from top left: This noodle vendor has carried her entire kit to this spot suspended from either end of a bamboo shoulder pole; A canal noodle vendor has festooned the bow of her boat with bananas and flowers as offerings to water deities; Wheeled vendor carts can be moved to any convenient location in the city; Miang kham is a tasty snack of ginger, dried shrimp, chilies, peanuts, coconut flakes, shallots and a sugarcane-shrimp sauce.

central market still does a brisk trade in fabrics from all over the world.

Culinary delights purveyed by street hawker stalls are one of the capital's biggest attractions, and you'll find no greater concentration—and none of better quality—of hawker foods than in Bangkok's Chinatown.

Follow the sound of clanging hammers and odor of welding to penetrate one of the capital's last surviving handicraft enclaves, Ban Baht, down a *soi*, or lane, off Boriphat Road. The last of three villages originally established by Rama I for this purpose, households in Ban Baht forge baht, black metal bowls carried from door to door by Thai monks every morning to receive alms-food from the Buddhist faithful. After hammering the bowls together from eight separate pieces of steel said to represent Buddhism's Eightfold Path, the smithies fuse the joints in a wood fire with bits of copper, then polish the bowl and coat it with several layers of black lacquer. Only a little farther north, Boriphat Road joins Bamrung Muang Road, which is lined with shops selling the monks bowls as well as bright ochre robes, meditation cushions and other monastic paraphernalia.

Bangkok was born of commerce, and the city abounds in historic markets running the gamut from diminutive to colossal. The city's most famous market, heavily visited by

Left: Sharply pointed gables and swooping rooflines are characteristic of traditional central Thai houses. Today such houses are extremely rare and highly coveted.
Right: The teak house of the late Jim Thompson, an American architect who revived Thailand's silk industry in the 1960s, is now one of Bangkok's most enduring attractions.

local residents as well as visitors, is the Chatuchak Weekend Market, found near the Moh Chit Bus Terminal in northern Bangkok. Open only on Saturday and Sunday, close to 9,000 vendor stalls packed together over 35 acres (14 hectares) serve up to 200,000 visitors per day. Everything imaginable is on hand at Chatuchak, including antiques, rustic wooden furniture, ceramics, the latest in trendy Thai-designed clothing, antiquarian books, Thai musical instruments, wickerware, Thai silks, hill-tribe handicrafts, Buddhist amulets, fine art and military surplus gear.

Opposite Lumpini Park, a newer market called Suan Lum doesn't get started till after dark, pulling together a collection of booths offering bargains on everything from jewelry and handicrafts to cowboy hats and tattoos. Beer gardens and Thai hawker stalls ensure no one need leave the complex for sustenance till all one's shopping needs have been sated.

More upscale shopping is available in several spots around the city, most conveniently in the seemingly endless string of department stores and shopping arcades stretched from Siam Square to Sukhumvit Road.

Children visiting the City of Angels delight in the animal attractions at Samut Prakan Crocodile Farm, home to over 30,000 crocodiles, and the Dusit Zoo, a former private botanical gardens for Rama V converted to exhibit one of the best zoological collections in Southeast Asia.

Left: Muang Boran, a historical park southwest of Bangkok in Samut Prakan, contains a scale replica of Sanphet Prasat palace.
Right: The Muang Boran complex, also known as Ancient City, includes replicated architecture from all over Thailand, such as this northern Thai-style temple.

Clockwise from top left: Vimanmek Mansion, the largest teak building in the world, was built in the 19th century as a palace for King Rama V. Today it is a much-visited museum; Vimanmek is filled with both Thai and European antiques; King Rama V's royal reception room at Vimanmek; One of several other royal buildings constructed of teak in the Victorian style on the grounds of Vimanmek.

The exquisite Lacquer Pavilion at Bangkok's Suan Pakkat palace dates to the Ayuthaya period and features gold-leaf *jataka* (Buddha's past lives) and Ramayana murals applied to black lacquer.

Meanwhile the city's burgeoning fine and popular arts scene provides us with an everyday-changing social landscape of beauty, inspiration and challenge. Over 200 art galleries host rotating exhibitions of visual arts from both Thai and foreign artists. Public art has never been more popular than at any time in Bangkok's history, with daring neo-traditional designs and color schemes on restaurant walls, temple murals and anywhere else artists can find space.

The plastic arts, especially architecture, also thrive in this city that has been moving skywards almost as fast as it has expanded outwards. When the Dusit Thani Hotel opened in 1970 it was the capital's tallest building; by the end of that decade fewer than 25 buildings stood taller than six floors. By the time the new millennium came along, nearly a thousand buildings could claim that distinction, with at least 20 of them towering higher than 45 floors. Proclaiming its monumental verticality like a colossal exclamation point, the 60-story Thai Wah II building on Sathon Tai Road combines rectangles and squares to create a geometric mosaic style updating Egyptian Deco. The nearby Bank of Asia headquarters, known locally as the "Robot Building," combines nut-and-bolt motifs at various elevations with a pair of lightning rods on the roof (arranged to resemble sci-fi robot-like antennae) and two metallic-lidded 'eyes' staring out from the structure's upper façade.

Left: The Oriental Hotel, located along the Chao Phraya River, is one of the world's most luxurious hotels.
Right: The Sala Rim Naam restaurant, located in the Oriental Hotel, takes advantage of traditional Thai temple motifs to provide atmosphere.

Left: Modern spas in Bangkok make ample use of Thailand's ancient healing techniques.
Above: Facials may incorporate ingredients from Thai traditional medicine's vast repertoire of herbal treatments.
Right: Thai massage blends together elements of deep tissue massage, yoga and soothing strokes.

Such pure verticality is now giving way to tiered skyscrapers in accordance with the city's setback regulations for allowing light onto city streets. The ziggurat-shaped Sathorn City Tower stacks marble, glass and granite around recessed entryways and window lines to create a spectacular Mesopotamia-meets-Madison Avenue effect. Everything 'neo' is in, including the new neo-Thai architecture sweeping the city. The Regent, The Sukhothai and the Grand Hyatt Erawan are all examples of hotels that make extensive use of Thai classical motifs in both layout and ornamentation.

Bangkok's relatively new self-consciousness as expressed in the arts has helped to boost urban pride, which in turn has led Bangkokians to put more thought into urban planning issues. Realizing that late 20th-century development changed the shape of Bangkok forever, residents are now looking towards the future with an eye to doing whatever possible to make their city a more pleasant and efficient place to work and live in.

To relieve the lack of surface streets, the city installed a system of elevated freeways that now enable commuters to leapfrog the traffic congestion below. In 1999 the city unveiled the Skytrain, an elevated rail network that has made a sizeable dent in Bangkok traffic and allowed a large number of city residents to switch from the slow, often crowded city bus system. One unexpected benefit to the new system is that riding the Skytrain raises everyone 12 meters

Left: Bangkok's go-go bars make up part of the city's legendary nightlife.
Right: Bangkok's transvestite cabaret shows are a popular tourist draw.

(40 feet) above street level, affording glimpses of lush greenery and old Bangkok architecture not ordinarily visible below due to high walls. Many Bangkokians, during the first year of the Skytrain's debut, expressed surprise that their city was actually more attractive than they'd previously believed.

The latest boon to city transport, the MRTA subway, links the "old Bangkok" of Chinatown, Hualamphong and Banglamphu with the "new Bangkok" further east along Sukhumvit Road, the city's longest and broadest thoroughfare. Despite the once-popular sentiment that it couldn't be done, engineers dug the MRTA tunnels 23 meters (75 feet) below street level using the same techniques as used for the channel tunnel between France and Great Britain.

Concurrent with the ongoing growth of concrete, steel and asphalt, there exists a countering if not equal movement in the development of green areas and public parks in Bangkok. Lumphini Park—Suan Lum in local parlance—is the city's oldest and until recently the largest, with 144 acres (60 hectares) of grass, trees and an artificial lake, all very close to the city center. A major recreational focus for people living in the older districts near the Chao Phraya River, the park teems with people in the morning practicing tai chi, jogging or just taking a nap in the shade. On weekends during the cool season, the 80-piece Bangkok Symphony Orchestra performs, drawing classical music lovers from all over the city.

Left: Several entertainment parks on the outskirts of Bangkok offer the opportunity for close encounters with elephants.
Right: Over 30,000 crocodiles call the Samut Prakan Crocodile Farm home. Tourists crowd the farm daily to watch the feeding of the crocodiles and other animals.

Rama IX Park, at 200 acres (80 hectares) now the city's largest, is well known for its well-tended collection of outdoor tropical flora as well as greenhouses filled with rare plants from around the world. Off Sri Nakarin Road in the newer eastern side of the city, Rama IX Park is popular on weekends, yet nearly deserted during the week.

The latest Bangkok trend towards greenness is to develop pocket parks in unused and undeveloped areas of the city. Both of Bangkok's two surviving 18th-century forts, Phra Sumen and Mahakan, have had adjacent lots planted with grass and trees to provide urbanites relief from their mostly concrete-glass-and-steel existence.

All of these brave movements towards the city's future, whether in art, mass transport or urban planning, signal a new optimism for Bangkok. It's not unusual nowadays to speak with a native Bangkokian who may comment, "Ten years ago I was looking for another place to live in Thailand. Now I think I'll stay."

Left and right: Pattaya, just over an hour's drive southeast of Bangkok, provides a Miami Beach-like experience of resorts, tourist shops and body-packed beaches.

Clockwise from top left: Hua Hin's charming teak railway station was originally built for royal visits to the seaside; The broad, shallow beaches of Hua Hin are perfect for all-day lounging; Hua Hin boasts the traditional *samlor* or three-wheeled pedicab as well as the more modern motorized version, called *tuk-tuk* by foreigners for the sound of their two-stroke engines; The Central Sofitel resort is famous for its topiary gardens.

Right: A slender standing Buddha and monastic cells flank a boulder-studded hill at a monastery near Hua Hin.

SELECTED FURTHER READING

A gilded *kinnari*, a mythical half-human, half-bird creature from Hindu-Buddhist mytholodgy, extends a flower in offering to the Buddha at Wat Phra Kaew.

Bangkok: Angelic Illusions, Barry Bell (Reaktion Books 2003)

Bangkok: Place, Practice and Representation, Marc Askew (Routledge 2002)

Bangkok: The Story of a City, Alec Waugh (W. H. Allen 1970)

Bangkok, Vol. 1 William Warren (Consortium 2002)

Buddhism Explained, Laurence-Khantipalo Mills, (Silkworm 1999)

Bangkok 8, John Burdett (Random House 2003)

Thai Style, William Warren (Rizzoli 1989)

Four Reigns, Kukrit Pramoj (Silkworm 1999)

Toward a Social History of Bangkok, Scott Barne (Rowman & Littlefield Publishers 2002)

The Intimate Economies of Bangkok: Tomboys, Tycoons, and Avon Ladies in the Global City, Ara Wilson (University of California 2004)

Jasmine Nights, SP Somtow (St Martins 1995)

Nine Temples of Bangkok, Helen Bruce (Progress 1960)

Old Bangkok, Michael Smithies (Oxford University 2004)

The Balancing Act: A History of Modern Thailand, Joseph Wright Jr (Asia Books 1991)

A Woman of Bangkok, Jack Reynolds (Ballantine Books 1968)

Reflections on Thai Culture, William Klausner (Siam Society 1993)

The Making Of Modern Bangkok, Marc Askew (Jomtien 1993)

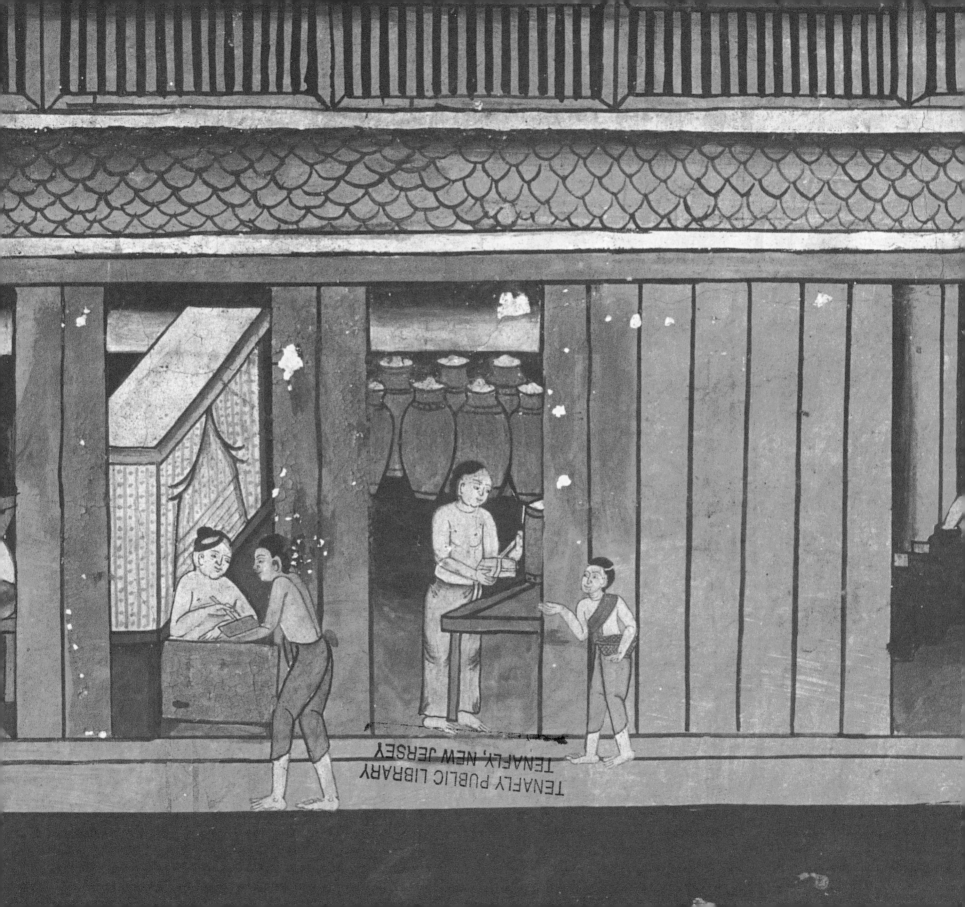